POETRY

372

THE
EMPEROR HEART

Also by Laurence Whistler

———

ARMED OCTOBER AND OTHER POEMS (1932)
FOUR WALLS (1934)

THE
EMPEROR HEART

Laurence Whistler

Decorated by
REX WHISTLER

NEW YORK

The Macmillan Company

MCMXXXVII

PRINTED IN THE UNITED STATES OF AMERICA
BY THE POLYGRAPHIC COMPANY OF AMERICA, N.Y.

FOR
URSULA

Some of these poems have already appeared in *The London Mercury, Life and Letters, The New Oxford Outlook, The Poetry Review, The Observer, John O' London's Weekly* and *Nash's Magazine,* and acknowledgments are due to the editors. Also to Father D'Arcy, S. J., with regard to an inscription at Campion Hall, Oxford.

PREFACE

THIS is the third book of poems by Laurence Whistler. It is always a deep pleasure to find in the second and third books of any writer a growth of mind, a widening of range, with new tuning and toning of the instrument.

Often, a first book will contain all the enthusiasms and delights of a young writer's twenty years. It will seem to be abundant. His second book, published a year later, being a record of the fewer delights of only one year, may seem to be thin and disappointing. Then, his third book, published a year later, being the record of the very few delights not already recorded, may seem to be the shadow of the books which came first. After this, too often, there is no fourth book. It becomes clear that it was not Poetry speaking in the young man, but Youth.

Like Browning's wise man, most students of poetry before they reach old age are able to say,

"I have known four-and-twenty leaders of revolts."

They will have seen geniuses hailed, fêted, then less fêted, then unnoticed, then dropped and forgotten, while others take their places. It is only the rare soul who matures. As a rule, it is Youth that has been vocal in these geniuses, not poetry.

When I read Laurence Whistler's first book, I was sure that it was the book of one in whom a spirit of poetry was speaking, and that this spirit of poetry, being, like all such in a young man of promise, a wistful and beautiful thing, full of strange and unusual life, would show growth upon its next appearance. I was not disappointed. It did show growth, in the happiest possible way. There was a growth of structure; the new poem was on bigger and stronger lines than anything in the first book; it was a big conception, well and manfully carried through. It seemed to me to be on a nobler design than any poem written by a man under thirty since the War.

In this, his third book, there is a new advance, not, this time, in the choice of fable and power of construction, but in the stuff and fabric of the poems, their imagery, thought and language. The verse, in this book, is surer and finer. It has become a personal thing, a style of Laurence Whistler's own, unlike the writing of any other. It is a choice style, musical, skilful, and in the best of the English method. Where he sees the chance of making a new effect, he makes it. Like a sensible poet, he aims at enriching the method of his race, and will not fling away that which has served beauty lastingly because it dates from of old.

Laurence Whistler's thought is occupied with beauty. He finds it in the sense that the dead of his race abide here with living qualities of grace and truth which touch us in moments of emotion; in many charming and delicate broodings on the passion of love; and newly and thrillingly in some understanding poems about the souls of old and famous houses, ruined or in use, on which character has been stamped by architect or occupier.

The book has given me much pleasure. It seems to me to be the work of one with a mind of delicate beauty, a style both precise and fastidious, a preoccupation with the thoughts roused by high emotion and with that rarer quality of becoming more of a poet as he grows older. We are rich in young poets at this time. Laurence Whistler is one of those whose work we shall watch with the keenest expectation. In the meantime, he has fulfilled all our hopes with this book of exquisite and thrilling poems.

JOHN MASEFIELD.

CONTENTS

CONTENTS

QUAINTON CHURCHYARD

I kneel in sunlight, lifting to a stone
A hand made sensitive to love and pain,
This thing of gentle crimson and warm bone
To learn the sorrow a few words contain,
And pick at the vanished capitals in the stone.
Nerves upon sunlit emptiness, in vain.
   Only a cherub looks into the air
   Keeping the secret from me without guile:
   He has forgotten why his lips still wear
   The obliterated sweetness of a smile.
The burning stone against my finger tips
Is only burning stone for all they do,
   They never will get nearer to
The original sorrow in those smiling lips.

[1]

Lover or happy husband lusty and tall,
Or pale consumptive girl by neighbours heard
All one winter coughing through the wall,
Or lonely child with thin cheeks like a bird,
Sweet bones that April kept for ever small,
Whoever's lost in this green, natured word,
　　Listen, for one is kneeling to you, one
　　You know, in all identical with you,
　　If he were not a little more in the sun,
　　Oh if I know this day one thing you knew—
The eye of evening blue on wall and hill—
That dog for ever crying at his post
　　Among the windy pastures lost—
Speak to me, ghost! in burning England still.

But only a wind, whose speech I cannot trace,
Between the living darkness of the yews
Speaks to those pinnacles of ancient race—
And here the living beautiful shadow grows
Along the cheek of this beguiling face,
Or edges into nothing, I suppose.
　　Someone brought into the world with crying
　　To wake and dream and call it all his own
　　This which I cannot waken with my crying,
　　A little sad brown hair and dreamless bone.

But now the wind from luminous bough to bough
All silk of faithless summer has unfurled—
   Here is the true, consoling world,
Which having youth and dreams, I call my own.

Oh keep me chaste in action: chastity
Is the bright eye of unbetrayed desire
And the clear voice of passion. Set in me
That Easter voice my countrymen require
Who seem to hang at last upon their hour
Of perilous Spring, all holding breath to see
Petrol of Europe by a naked fire!
   Give us that harmony of blood that ran
     Through the great days of action and of song
     Into the confident majesty of man.
And now for all true men and women I pray;
Give us that golden balance of the strong
   To which alone true joys belong
In the short fiery sweetness of our day.

THE STRANGE COMEDY

Here's a sweet comedy. 'T begins with O
Dolentis and concludes with ha, ha, he!

After the clock that ticks away the day
Solemn to children in the shadowy hall
Has kept twelve hours all our goings on
Within a strict and dictatorial sway;
After my naked character through all
Has suffered armour of normality,
And crossed its dagger with each minute and won
The approved and empty poise of decency,
An uncle or a gentleman or son,
For growth inflicts these many masks on one;
When only in the rooms the breath of hay
Remains while evening on the blue witch-ball
Has dwindled to a point of silver light,
And dew and darkness for the spirit fall—

Then pleased another hateful day has gone,
And lonely, listening for a ghost of you
In this old room of locked, familiar night
Where you have slept as the walls know too well,
I climb into my bed and all my fighting's done
And having no white arms to go into,

I go unarmed into the sheets alone,
Wishing, through all my wishing, to become
The blissful prince again that I once was
When I kept palace in my mother's womb.

They say I only come to you because
I would return to that one simple joy
Of marvellous nothing nearest to a tomb;
But a warm tomb. They say the enchanted girl
Assumes that passionate longing of the boy—
And you are made a beacon in my sea,
The light at which for ever now I'll steam,
Harbour of home and end of odyssey
Where in my loneliest night I tread in dream,
Only that our two loves of such a force,
So near, so generous, palpable, proud, sweet,
May start one night on its tremendous course
Our spit and image, racing with unknown feet
Poor child, through heaven where no pain can be
In your discreet and dreamless beauty lying,
To launch alone into an icy sea
Stark in the winds of pain for ever flying.

They say this of us, knowing you and me
Much better than ourselves, these learned men;

That we who are the eloquence of youth
Seek only to be soundless babes again.
We know their testimony is the truth.
Yet strange, that when our beauties flame, and they
Approach from kiss to kiss the gorgeous Mass
That the same night redeems the world, they lay
The simple supper of our ecstasy
All for a phantom uninvited guest!
That though we spend and ravish time away
While the pale Crown adorns the chimney pot
All we are seeking actually is rest,
With arms that murder rest!
                                        Strange comedy,
When all desire unquenchable and hot
Can only nudge in each a craving deep
To go that voyage to another room
And twenty years to a forgotten womb,
Each to an ageing woman light of sleep
Who listens to the silence while she prays
Like the pure moon that called her to its light,
The passionless fire upon the saintly gaze
Quite still; quite spent; dead beauty's famished urn
Near whom love's feet, maybe, have passed and will
          return
Ruled by the clock that ticks away the night.

[6]

LODGE AND MANSION

When you have left me, beautiful, alone,
This tireless soul and tired thing of breath,
Again toward two houses I must run
And always be encroaching fast upon
Your beauty and the hour of my death.

How little, in your loving if I died
Kissed into Silence, should I want of faith!
But like an artless bridegroom and a bride
Never my resolutions coincide—
Your beauty and the hour of my death.

Oh then some darkness when delight is due
Conceal in your rare lips a painless wraith
Of poison to consume my body too,
That I may drink, while all the world is you,
Your beauty and the hour of my death.

Then under holy arms what could we fear?
We would not fear, to do no more with breath.
It was the curious dawn we could not bear
That looked into the night—oh take, my dear,
Your hour and the beauty of my death.

[7]

CHATTERTON AND YOU AND ME

Chatterton before he killed himself
Danced seventeen times around a minor star
On a great stone still fiery at the core,
Poor boy if he had waited for ten dances more
He would have been where the Eternal are.
The sparrows now, he heard,
Are remote dignified ancestors; his bones
Crumbled into London; every word
Said then in London forgotten. But the stones
He kicked, our children's children's child shall fall
And graze a knee and bruise on them a bone.

[8]

And he and we and golden lovers all
Go dancing on the Earth, a whirling stone
About a fiery star;
When some feel tired
Always happy dancers waiting are.
This way the world renews its capital.

. . . She entered with a frost of rain
That glittered in the firelit air
On blown hair, her blown bright hair,
And lay in flakes across her hands
And scattered petals blown upon her cheeks,
It was almost pain
For him to breathe the known heart of her hair
And the breath of the dark streets on her.
Two then were one,
One who could ask no more of living, or dying
For him: he was in Eden gates again
And he would love her, he was crying,
Alway, even unto the end of the world . . .

He said this. This was done
Many centuries ago: as many beyond to-morrow.
Time's insignificant. Stones
Are lasting, they are stronger than bones.

Lovers are no more than the instant joy and sorrow
They feel. A bright match carried in a catacomb.
A length of fiery being by the clock.
They are not even lasting as their bones.
Think upon stones.

GOOD FRIDAY

It was that season when on earth
Love in all living things has birth
And laughing fires of lust pursue
The fox on the down, the worm in dew,—
When love distils the darting wing
To a dark shadow, that is Spring.
And then one morning it was heard:
The loud axe, like an uncouth bird.
And plainly in three meadows round
When it had stopped the sinister sound
Of a great saw going to and fro
Like a Puritan singing, dark and slow.
Yet there four genial men were come,
Parmenter, Orchard, Elwood, Tom,
With murderous easy minds to fell
Summer's corinthian capital,
An elm that had two hundred years
In its gold mournful fronds the stars,
The night these fellows were begot
Or nightmare-haunted in a cot.
Proud doom, so small a starlit face
Dreaming on cottage springs should grow
To wish the pillar of time's grace
To a low grave, and lay it low;

For soon it brought down all its hours
With a loud voice into the flowers,
And it was finished. —Tom's wild boot
Raped the enchanted primrose root.
And then a cock raised up on high
His ancient and reminding cry,
And churches in the valley told,
Dark in the towers, their tumbling gold.

That night, about the hour went down
Flashing in twigs the quiet sun,
There sprang upon the Irish Sea
A loud wind ignorant of this tree.
But at midnight it was decrying,
Into all dreams' believing ears,
Some evil thing, some death or dying,
Whether in laughter or in tears.
So all night in the shivering joists
It whistled the poor ignorant mouse
And shut up sleep into the house
(Sleep of the living, stare of ghosts)
With all the moans and musics slight
That comfort and alarm the night.
And then, with dawn, all day aloud
It ran and raced its hurrying cloud,

A wind that crossed too quick for rain
The solemn wilderness of the plain.
Yet once along a distant hill
There went at noon one tenuous frill
Of muslin sunlight for a minute,
And so it faded—like the vain
Small flutter from a fading train .
That takes too much of living in it.

The second day at fall of night
I could not think, nor read, nor write,
The wind discoursing to my brain
In cowl and chimney, and in pane.
I went out in the gusty dark
To see how that long corpse would look,
But had not thought the moon was whirling
Mottled-white like a new shilling—
Across the hill her light flew on
From hedge to hedge, and so was gone.
The wind-flowers then obscure and chill
Would offer their weak light, but still
In and out the curious moon
Hung flashing, like a silver spoon.
The moon and a great darkness edged
With fiery ermine flew together—

Beyond the impact, wild and smudged
Her face went on in troubled weather.—
I saw as that eclipse began
Rise up the figure of a man
Among the branches, ghost or human,
I could not tell, a man or woman,
The shape of a lamenting man
Among the branches.—Was it Pan
Mourning from his grave in the sun
For in an hour's empty act
The journey of much beauty's done,
Crying, with his syrinx cracked?
Was it some harsh thin-lipped Saint
Who made a pulpit of those boughs
And them his ghastly text, to paint
A picture of my heart's cracked vows?—
Such fancies kept my mind engrossed
Because I knew it was the ghost
Of that dear woman's love that blind
I murdered with untroubled mind.

THE SEPULCHRE

Now is the time between Good Friday and
Easter. We're absolutely in the tomb.
                              —D. H. LAWRENCE.

I rouse at windy four
From something I said in a dream,
To the sad darkness of four—
A train's forgotten scream,
The sad ordinary wind,
All things known before,
Darkness we share no more,
With dawn grey in the wind,
Lying together no more;
And pluck at the crumpled shroud,
And enter a grave dream
Murmuring your beautiful name
Without hope of an answer, aloud.

EASTER

The corn is moved a little on this hill,
The sun embellishing the youthful corn,
The lambs at ending of their frolics, still
Cry in the darkened valleys where they run,
The robins' children in the whispering thorn
Forget their hunger with the falling sun—
And in her lap I lay my forehead down
So near the child unborn, time's happy bud,
That is all loves of bird and beast in one,
All April in the temple of her blood.

O put my arms about the vernal waist
And close my eyes upon the immortal womb.
Rest, rest, distracted frame, against the core
Of all this darkening love that is your home—
The many heart-beats in one silent nest,
The lambs still crying in the English hills,
The corn on the hill, and the wind over the corn:
And rest beloved, rest, and fear no more:
No ill in time to come most full of ills
Can wash away the beauty of being born.

A BED IN STARLIGHT

I see her now a dancing Fury
    With a hate too wild to bear,
    Fiery cheeks and frosty scorn
    Of bright eyes and brighter hair,
    Like a drop upon a thorn
Dancing to a flash of glory.

I see her now a softly-straying
    Angel in my firelit room,
    Her faint wings of loving made—
    The only love in the world to whom
    This year I ever knelt and prayed
At any time when I was praying.

I see her, oh I see a woman
    Who has loved and hated me
    For an earthly season, she
    Into whose dark love I creep
    Softly, to preserve asleep
All I'll get of God or human.

JOHN DELAFIELD

John Delafield looked up from Adam Bede
And saw the platform and enormous name
Flow by him in the empty sunlight like a dream.
But his alighting no one came
To welcome, with the smile of host or love,
The very meaning of
The song of the blackbird and the escaping steam.

He crossed the wooden bridge behind another,
And saw the low hills very blue from rain
And the steam blowing over them like petals,
And there beneath him the long train
Ready to resume its wandering
Into the heart of Spring
For miles of silver evening on the metals.

John Delafield walked up the narrow street,
Invisible lilac of nobility
About his heart, for suffering is the rain
That grows the blossoming lilac-tree.
A youth unnoticed in the sleepy square
Born to enrich this air,
Or lie upon a battle-field in pain.

So to pass time he took that quiet lane
Into the darkening churchyard, still with Spring,
And into the dark church that gathered there
Always perhaps that gathering,
And knelt in the musty chapel with those five
Women who turned as if
A little astonished that he should kneel in prayer.

He knelt and stood and listened to the words
And held his peace there once with those poor souls.
But long ago they went into the night,
The doors are locked, the dark hours cold,
The kettle sleeps upon the pitiful ring.
The dear moon crying with a little light
Looks in the woods of England, dim with Spring.
O Love of God, be with and shield
The soul and body of John Delafield.

THE ENIGMA

Man, what is man? A hasty tool
Forged in four seconds of distracted fire,
Unkindly cast into the world to cool
In the cold wind of loneliness, until
Bracing his metal to the wind reveal
The beauty of his spirit and desire,
As every quality of edge and steel
Soul, the delighted craftsman, can require!

Man, what is man? The Prince of Time,
The roof of the world, and cornice of renown,
Whose thoughts go up into the stars of rhyme
Or flit between the Scorpion and the Crown—
And whose most daring act is to uncover,
To the indifferent ear of darkness, all
His little failures to be loved or lover,
Crying between the pillow and the wall.

Man, what is man but woman's toy,
Needing her hands at first in pitiful harms,
Humbled all his life to need the joy
That's in one woman or another's arms;
And even in the grave I dare say lonely
Till the dark fingers of the trees break through—
Woman, you make us at your pleasure, only
That our strong bones may be embraced by yew.

PAN TO SYRINX

My dear, if it distresses you
I only love you as I do,
And all my simple passion said
Served but to make you share your bed
With grief not me, if this is so
You should not walk about you know
In that sweet body and bright hair
Designed at large to tantalise,
Nor use so freely everywhere
The slanting darkness of your eyes.

You've not one inch of beautiful flesh
But's there to arouse and grant my wish.
My dear, a million years ago
The proud and bountiful sun we know
Who looks with equal love upon
The peacock and the puritan
Gave you gold head and liquid waist
Like a bright snake for you to taste
The infinite pleasure in this use,
Though he'll not frown if you refuse.

THE GHOST NEVER BREATHED OF

On Christmas Eve as Rupert lay
  Stretched in the guest bed dim
He thought a ghost came to his side
  And faintly looked at him.

He saw the ghost of a pale girl
  Move softly through the room,
And by the feeble square of stars
  The gold on her temple bloom.

"Last year they put me in that place,
  Rupert, if you but knew
How cold and narrow a bed is mine
  You'd let me stay with you."

She's slipped between the glowing sheets
  Ashiver with the chill,
And put a mouth upon his mouth,
  And so she has her will.

And swiftly at the touch of love
　　Her veins take fire and glow—
And ever the clock in the hall cried out
　　Through its dark mistletoe.

Then faint and far away the cock
　　Crew small in Pityme Farm:
She turned her in the twilight room,
　　That body so true and warm.

The cocks all crew to tell poor ghosts
　　To rid the world of harm,
Loud beneath the ashen hill
　　And faint in Pityme Farm.

She started softly in a dream
　　And in a dream turned over,
Her heart was full of sweet red blood—
　　She would not leave her lover.

That body was full of sweet red blood
    That dreamed in the peep of day,
All made of lovable perishing stuff
    In the world's fine way.

Now lovely creatures the whole earth over
    Who dream of your desire
Prize the stuff of your warm bright flesh
    That's tinder to love's fire.

Prize the merry heat of youth
    And the light of your eyes' glancing,
Your heart so full of sweet red blood
    That never leaves his dancing.

It may be ghosts this very dawn
    Upon your roof-tops go,
Their life a fading looking-glass
    Of all they cherished so.

Troubled eyes a moment seen
    Searching a vanished drawer:
Lips thin as the ghost of a rose
    For kissing any more.

Blown from the grey edge of the globe
    At the psalm of a red bird,
That creeps through sash and casement far,
    Unheard or hardly heard.

Blown, blown in the aching wind
    At a sound in the dark shires,
A gust of feeble shivering straws
    Blown past the ashen spires.

SHOTOVER HILL, OXFORDSHIRE

This wind enveloping my sunlit hand
Is blowing flowers on the fading hills
And blowing golden evening up the land
Out of the clappers of Atlantic bells.
Mad with this music fresh in the mind and raging
Over the cowls of Bridgwater and Bath
And up the Severn Estuary rampaging
It drove into the delicate hills its path
Of hurrying silver; till about the sky
And blown about a hundred veering cocks,

Gloucestershire chiming gently in its clocks,
It puffed from towers the rhyming hours awry
High over Rectory yews, and all unheard
By postman at the pillar-box and parson
Wrestling to-morrow's sermon with the Word.
This wind upon the Cotswolds streaming blind
For Shotover and me split in its thirst
Round Radcliffe's noble bubble of the mind
Where still perhaps a little army stand
Of heroes never fated for a first—
And for a second, here, it cuffs my idle hand.

All, all a portion of an ancient land
Whose trophied glory trembles at to-morrow—
And all its flowers blowing over hills
And all its keyholes singing in the wind
The music of a house's joy or sorrow,
And all its people rich in ancient blood,
A history of beauty in the marrow,
Childish and wise and vicious and forlorn,
Those whom I love and hate for they are good,
And all its darkening hills where legions stood
And only cornflowers in the Roman corn
Can make a trophy of a rusted harrow.

This is indeed the very land of love,
Blind, growing blind now in a million panes
I cannot see—but only the first drove
Of lights, like starlings, flit across the plains.
And see in vision from another year
Another village in an evening's dust
And in the empty schoolroom's diamond panes
The little pots of fading maidenhair
Among the children's crooked texts put there
To cure a great world of its modern sorrow—
Pitiful and gentle as a crust
Eaten by a mongrel from a beggar's hand.—
And always through these things I see to-morrow
Like a still ruffian in an alley stand.

THE TOMB'S ALTERNATIVE

A Variation of The Sepulchre

Troubled in dreams I turn
For the stair to a room forgotten,
Because of profound concern
For a child's face in the pane
Of a tower empty and rotten;
Haunted in dreams I turn,
And then I am hearing again—
The sad, actual wind
Unconscious of a hearer,
The quiet tick of the clock
And the far voice of a cock
Calling something to mind
Unhappy, and then nearer
The stumble of cattle in stall,
The tap of the shepherd's stick
As the gleam of his lantern wick
Fades on the simple wall.

Oh it has called to mind
You and forgotten days,
Time with a button-hole

Of your bright and dangerous ways,
The light of your ardent soul
I had in compassion and passion;
The shadow of much weeping
For all you did in harm.—
Change with the changing fashion,
Sleep on where you are sleeping
In the crook of another's arm.

A VALEDICTION

O sleep that tears the coverlet of shame
On all we have denied, from hem to hem,
Sees what the world blames in us, and we blame,
Too old to care, too gentle to condemn;
Be gentle with these children, suffer them
Not on the hooves of nightmare to depart
Hurled into cockcrow with a pounding heart!

JUBILATE DEO

At dawn his fire was twinkling on the shore
And first they took him for a countryman,
An indistinct dark figure looking on.
Even then no meeting was like this before,
This meal that in a kind of dream began:
The shadow of three weeks lay on each man;
And then, with his strange questions he was gone.
   Gone, but returning shortly as a King,

And they for Glory, soaring in his train!
O ending emptiness of time take wing . . .
The world became a waiting-room of pain
After that last unhappy breakfasting.
But none of them set eyes on him again.

Now centuries of similar desire
Have cooled into the coffins of a Faith—
Great empty Naves inquiring of the stars.
A mother reading by a nursery fire
In whom ten thousand years of love draw breath
Knows that no love or pain can outwit death:
Heaven and hell go by the window bars.
   Yet still two phantoms in her soul retain
The darkness where ten thousand years are furled;
The beautiful Spring God who died in pain,
The terror round the tree of knowledge curled:
Jesus from the world's foundation slain
And that old Serpent who deceives the world.

THE SICKBED

Her tired face upon the pillow lies,
The room's aflame with brimming bowl on bowl
Of all lordly and humble flowers. Her eyes
Brim with the visible flowers of her soul.

If this is pain to bloom like a rose-tree
Then keep this loved flesh in perpetual pain,
Or healing, and not healed, eternally,
As the sun gilds the roses through the rain.

THE GLASS CHANDELIER

The fire upon the books
Lifts its hurried looks:
It reads by tiny flames
The sad and golden names.
The wind at the window bars
Troubles the glass of stars.
The stars in the window pane
Alter like rain.

Fire, wind and star
Much in movement are.
Flesh of man the same—
Flash as star and flame
And faring like the wind
Now crowned with stars, now blind.
But wind cannot force,
Nor star to any course,
Though fire all night must show
The glass chandelier—
Like a larch in snow,
And a saint in air,
Or a very still lady.
A kind of beauty

Too near the look of death,
Too still, for us whose breath
Is troubled with desire
And brief as wind and fire.

THE ARCH OF LAUGHTER

The willows rage, the four winds blow,
The sun rolls out into the rain—
Across the winking fields below
Some casement flying to and fro
Catches his golden eye again:
A white cat skips in the village street
Arched upon her prancing feet:
The dog-fox in the shrubbery
Laughs at the Vicar's windy eye—
And over all, the rainbows rise
Reflecting fire to the skies,
Arc of the laughing earth rebuilt,
Hope's first unfailing archivolt:
A loop of flame before the wood,
A skein of flame into the cloud,
But where the cloud is rolled away
The merest shadow across the day.

Sweet God to be alive to taste
Air that the sun and rain have graced.
Thank the draughtsman stars, that drew
Earth on her faint ellipse, and you,
Merely for merry eyes to see

A white cat skip so delicately
Out of the wind she thinks no boon,
The wind lit up like Jubilee—
And if the politicians soon
Pull the roof about us, why,
Laugh at all things till you cry,
Civilisation's bleary eye,
And gaily at the world and die.

FEAR AT THE MANOR

Tuck me in, my darling Mother,
Tuck me in and all about,
I heard the Robber to-night laughing,
Nick in the Chimney laughing out.

I'll tuck you in, my little poppet,
I'll tuck you in and snugly too,
And then old Nick in the hall chimney
Shall never come to bother you.

Leave the door, my darling Mother,
Leave the door a little ajar,
Sometimes thinking makes me frightened
So many curious sounds there are.

I'll leave the door, my pretty robin,
I'll leave the door a good foot wide.
It's only the sea-wind at the windows
Or when the cock swings round outside.

Stay with me, my darling Mother,
Stay with me a little, for I,
I'm frightened when I think of dying,
Why were we made if we must die?

I'll stay with you, my own heart's treasure,
I'll climb your narrow bed into,
I'll hug you to my own warm body—
How should I know that more than you?

She stayed till he had lost all troubles,
And listened to his breathing low.

The doors shook, and a mouse laboured,
That storm four hundred years ago.

Four hundred years of changing Europe,
And grey lights on a grey house.
They have not made that changeless question
Any the easier for us.

FRANCIS FORTESCUE URQUHART

In a Book that was his Gift

Dear, honoured shade, now resting that calm head
In the cool morning of the recent dead,
Mild, constant star who lit with quiet mind
So many of the brilliant and the blind
That wrote this last and blotched, bewildered page
Bringing man's history to the present age;
Fond heart that gave me in one generous thought
All that four years to young distraction brought,
All joys in the grey town, much golden time
On Aphrodite spent, and much on rhyme;
What did my tongue or love unspoken say?—
For easily the heart of man can pay
All it is owing, oh most easily.
That which a man in simple dignity
Of a great debt will say, I left unsaid.
For which I mourn, and am not comforted.

Virtuous the gentle hand
    That moved upon this page for me,
And I desire these words may stand
    When I'm as dissolute as he.

FOUR NORTHERN HOUSES

*There being many more Valluable &
Agreeable things & Places to be Seen,
than in the Tame Sneaking South of England.*
                    —SIR JOHN VANBRUGH.

CASTLE HOWARD

Roll on, great Howard, through the gorgeous stars
Toward the golden fountain of the date,
Salute the Sun with capital and vase
And the vast heads upon your Satyr Gate.
Those looks compact of evil and delight
Full into morning fat with sunlight, roll,
As once you rolled them into fiery night
In the great storm when you received your soul !

When lightning traced you with his fingering flame,
Arch unto arch and cupola to ground,
And thunder all about your streaming frame
Ruined his monstrous Parthenons of sound,
Till you, that scraped acquaintance with the cloud,
Laughed out across your hissing lakes aloud!

LUMLEY CASTLE

It is four towers in a dripping park,
The signature of anarchy and awe—
And somewhere in the valley fourteen stark
Effigies of men I never saw.
Stained in the very stone with history,
In the sound in a gallery, wind in a flaw,
I cannot see it now but I must see
The fourteen men at church I never saw.

Now Vanbrugh made a rose of this dark house,
And they were many centuries dead the night
When he was but a kiss in candlelight.
His noble heart is in time's wolfish maw—
And still they shadow and importune us,
Those fourteen men at church I never saw.

SEATON DELAVAL

My head is sick, cries Seaton Delaval,
It must be fever from this bitter mould
Invents the tongues that clack in me and bawl;
For once I was too hot, but now am cold.
My head, my head, moans Seaton Delaval,
A great house to a colliery's dim ear.—
Yet, between you and me, in that dark hall
Pigeons alone will welcome you this year.

Laugh Vanbrugh! you whose laughs outlasted you:
A plaster statue and a poxy wit.
Lord Foppington has bowed the world adieu . . .
Up here, he knew the wind: would swear at it
Sawing his midnight sashes with blunt strife—
And then fire stained it like a surgeon's knife!

A CHARM FOR BLAGDON

No roving shadow of misfortune stain
The shadows that across your windows pass
In harmless glancing of the wind and rain
Or northern moonlight hurrying on your glass.
Nor fire look out of you with bloodshot eyes
Once, and bequeath a quiet skull to time.
Nor storm nor damp undo you.—I devise
This powerful charm and render it with rhyme.

No cloud of pain across your inward sun
The love that lights you darken or abate,
The light that dark or lit you have of one
Whose love and loveliness I celebrate.
Answer the looking in of sun and rain
With years of beauty looking out again.

FOUR INSCRIPTIONS

I

Written on a window pane at Campion Hall, Oxford

You who read this fickle page,
Illustrated by the sun,
Scribbled by the shower's rage,
Altering as the minutes run,
Think how alteration must
All endeavours bring to dust,
All that's mortal, man and house,
And of mercy, pray for us.

II

An Epitaph on Silver

Perfect they were in skill who fashioned me,
Every fine thing is made with artistry.
Rapacious rusty time on me must feed,
Do not all lovely things to this proceed?
I am not sad that I am early lit
To dust's faint bedroom, for all lie in it,
And in short measures life may perfect be.

III

Inscribed on a Bed at Blagdon, Northumberland

I do not question you, I am discreet,
Rich in experience, silent, & most sweet,
Only pour out your sorrows, sorrowing heart,
And I will heal them for I have the art;
Sweet lovers from your ancient play recall
Whatever scenes you will, I love them all.
I have known many things, love, birth & death,
And am grown gentle as my dreamers' breath.

IV

For a Pavilion in a Garden

To shadows make your pilgrimage, seek me when noon has
*   made*
A parched Arabia of the light, a Mecca of the shade;
And seek me when the showers drop their fading tapestries
Out of the rainbow's ruined arch on lawns & roofs & trees.
Here from the world's distraction come, for one green hour
*   find*
The quiet pulse, the wandering eye, the philosophic mind.

Here, children, spirit me away with make-believe and
   laughter,
And build me different in dreams upon dark pillows after.

NOTES

Shotover Hill, Oxfordshire (P. 28).—"Radcliffe's noble bubble" is the dome of the Radcliffe Library at Oxford.

Jubilate Deo (P. 34).—S. John xxi.

Castle Howard (P. 46).—The first of Sir John Vanbrugh's great undertakings in architecture; it was designed for the Earl of Carlisle in 1699. The outworks of Castle Howard include an arched gateway in the walled garden, flanked with squat pilasters, each bearing an immense Satyr's head.

Lumley Castle (P. 47).—The ancient four-towered castle of the Lumleys was modernized and embellished by Vanbrugh. More than a century before this, the neighbouring church of Chester-le-Street contained the fourteen recumbent effigies of the Lumleys, presenting, as it were, one contour of English history. It contains them still, I imagine.

Seaton Delaval (P. 48).—This house on the Northumberland coast, designed by Vanbrugh in 1718 for Admiral Delaval, was burnt out on the night of

January 3rd, 1822, and remains a blackened shell, inhabited only by birds, whose terrified commotion greets the visitor. Lord Foppington, the famous beau, appears in Vanbrugh's comedy, *The Relapse.*

A Charm for Blagdon (P. 49).—Written on a window pane at Blagdon, Northumberland.